Famous & Fun Deluxe Collection

21 Pieces from Famous & Fun:
Pop, Classics, Favorites, Rock, Duets

Carol Matz

Famous & Fun Deluxe Collection, Book 5, contains 21 well-loved selections drawn from the following books:

- Famous & Fun Pop, Book 5
- Famous & Fun Favorites, Book 5
- Famous & Fun Duets, Book 5
- Famous & Fun Classics, Book 5
- Famous & Fun Rock, Book 5
- Famous & Fun Pop Duets, Book 5

These teacher-tested arrangements are student favorites, and can be used as a supplement to any method. In addition to the wide variety of styles featured in this collection, a few equal-part (primo/secondo) duets are also included for students to have fun with ensemble playing.

Carol Matz

POP

Beauty and the Beast 8
The Imperial March (Darth Vader's Theme) . .14
New York, New York (Theme from) 5
Over the Rainbow 11
Under the Sea
 (from Walt Disney's *The Little Mermaid*) . . .2

CLASSICS

Canon (Pachelbel) 22
Clair de lune 26
Habanera (from the opera *Carmen*) 16
In the Hall of the Mountain King
 (from *Peer Gynt Suite*) 20
Un bel dì
 (from the opera *Madame Butterfly*) 18

FAVORITES

Alexander's Ragtime Band 32
America (My Country, 'Tis of Thee) 40
Maple Leaf Rag 29
The Star-Spangled Banner 38
Washington Post March 34

ROCK

Don't Stop Believin' 49
Eye of the Tiger 46
Imagine 42

DUETS

If I Only Had a Brain
 (from *The Wizard of Oz*) 56
James Bond Theme 60
Musetta's Waltz
 (from the opera *La bohème*) 52

Alfred

Produced by
Alfred Music
P.O. Box 10003
Van Nuys, CA 91410-0003
alfred.com

Printed in USA.

ISBN-10: 1-4706-1107-4
ISBN-13: 978-1-4706-1107-1

Under the Sea

(from Walt Disney's *The Little Mermaid*)

Lyrics by Howard Ashman
Music by Alan Menken
Arranged by Carol Matz

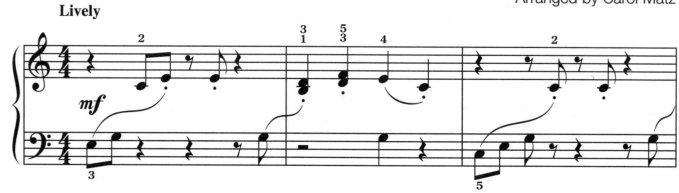

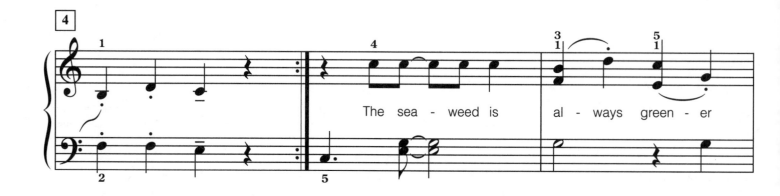

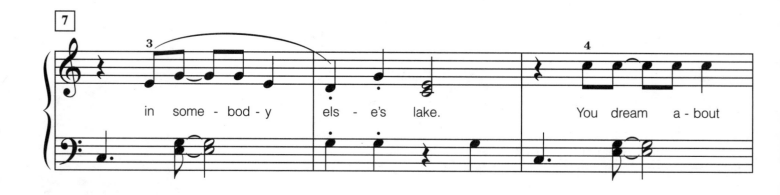

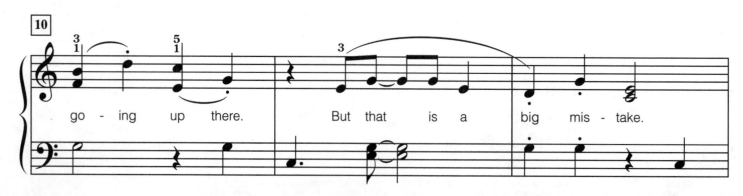

4

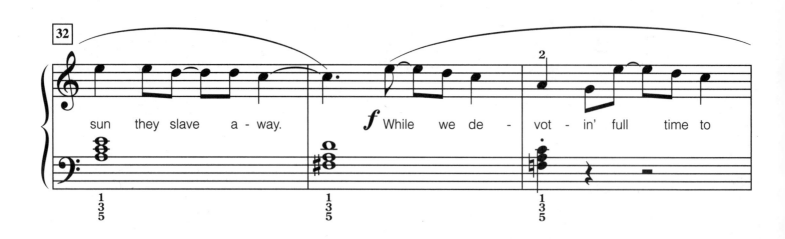

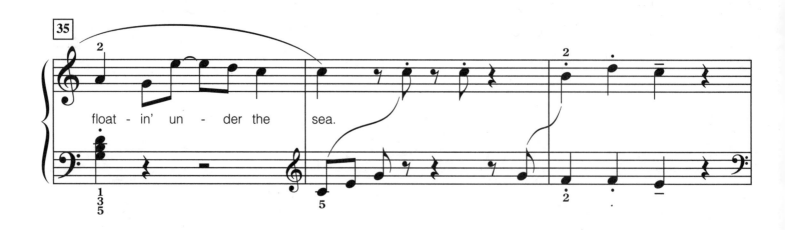

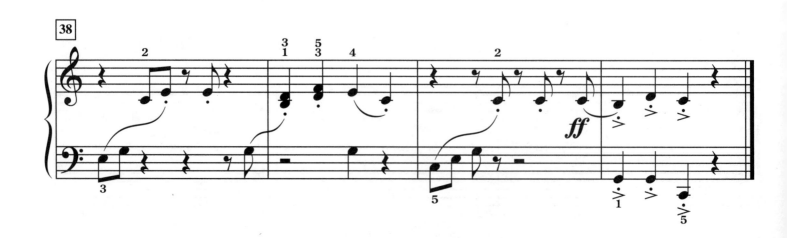

Theme from
New York, New York

Music by John Kander
Words by Fred Ebb
Arranged by Carol Matz

Beauty and the Beast

(from Walt Disney's *Beauty and the Beast*)

Words by Howard Ashman
Music by Alan Menken
Arranged by Carol Matz

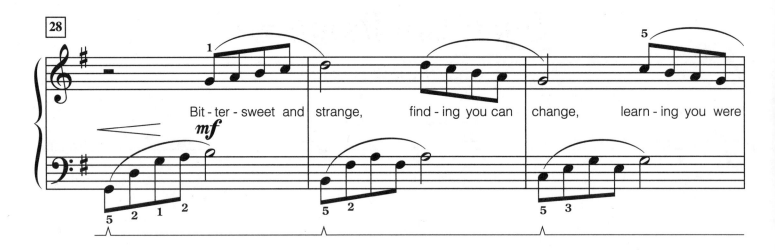

Bit - ter - sweet and strange, find - ing you can change, learn - ing you were

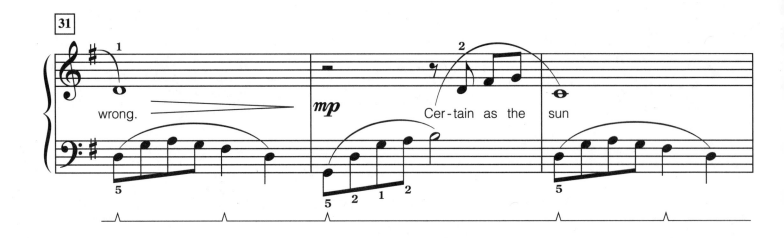

wrong. *mp* Cer - tain as the sun ris - ing in the

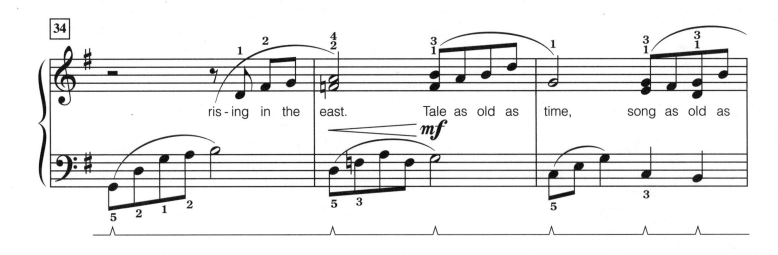

ris - ing in the east. Tale as old as time, song as old as

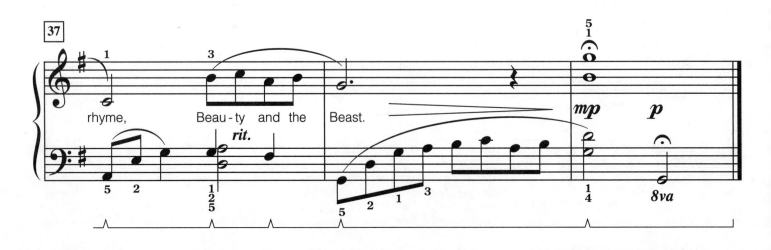

rhyme, Beau - ty and the Beast.

Over the Rainbow

(from *The Wizard of Oz*)

Music by Harold Arlen
Lyrics by E.Y. Harburg
Arranged by Carol Matz

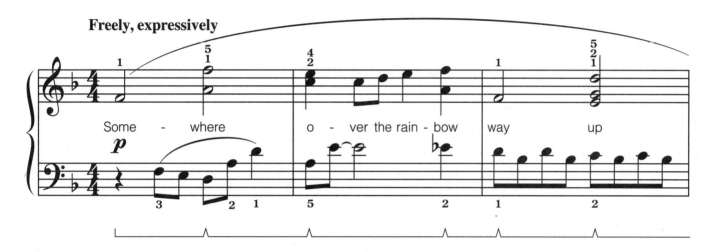

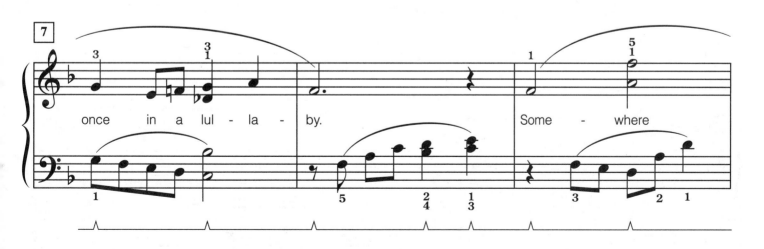

12

way a-bove the chim-ney tops, that's where you'll find me.

mf *rit.*

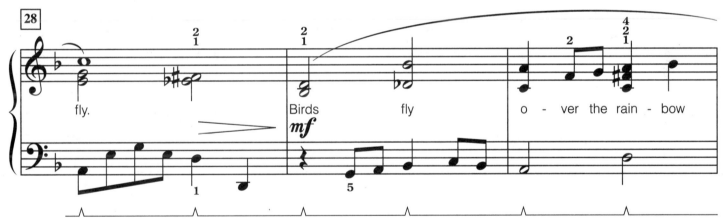

a tempo

Some - where o - ver the rain - bow blue - birds

f

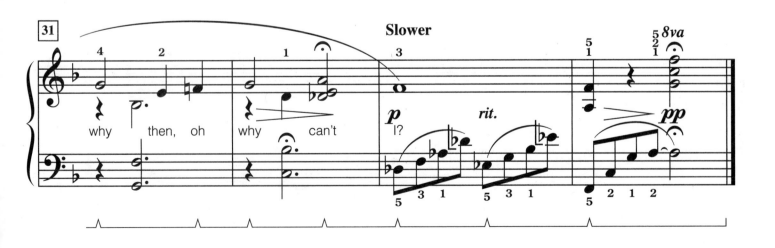

fly. Birds fly o - ver the rain - bow

mf

Slower

why then, oh why can't

p *rit.* *pp*

The Imperial March
(Darth Vader's Theme)
(from *Star Wars: The Empire Strikes Back*)

Music by **JOHN WILLIAMS**
Arranged by Carol Matz

Habanera

(from the opera *Carmen*)

Georges Bizet (1838–1875)
Arranged by Carol Matz

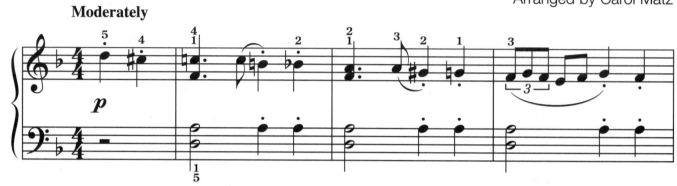

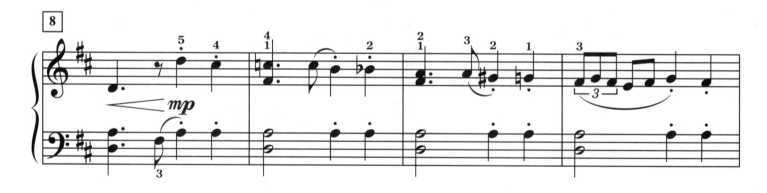

Un bel dì
(One Fine Day)

(from the opera *Madame Butterfly*)

Giacomo Puccini (1858–1924)
Arranged by Carol Matz

19

In the Hall of the Mountain King

(from *Peer Gynt Suite*)

Edvard Grieg (1843–1907)
Arranged by Carol Matz

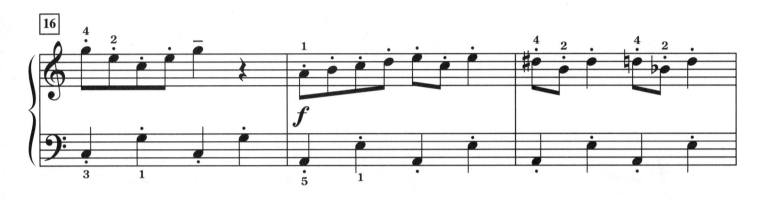

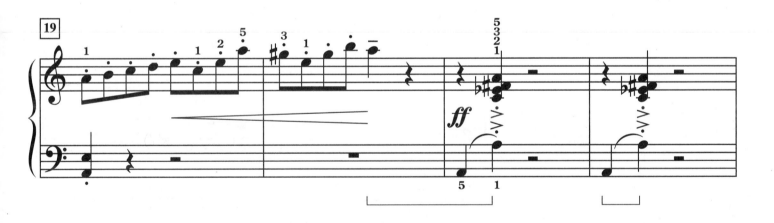

Canon

Johann Pachelbel (1653–1706)
Arranged by Carol Matz

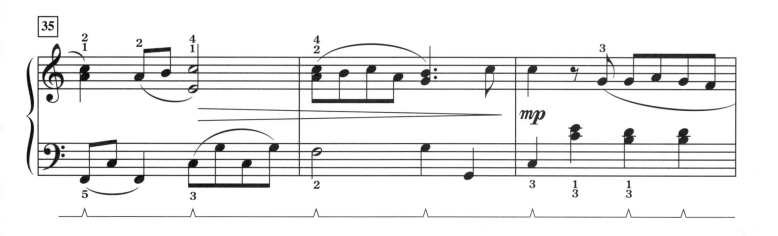

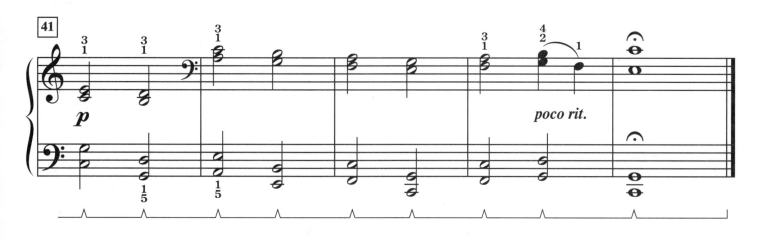

Clair de lune

(from *Suite bergamasque*)

Claude Debussy (1862–1918)
Arranged by Carol Matz

Moderately slow

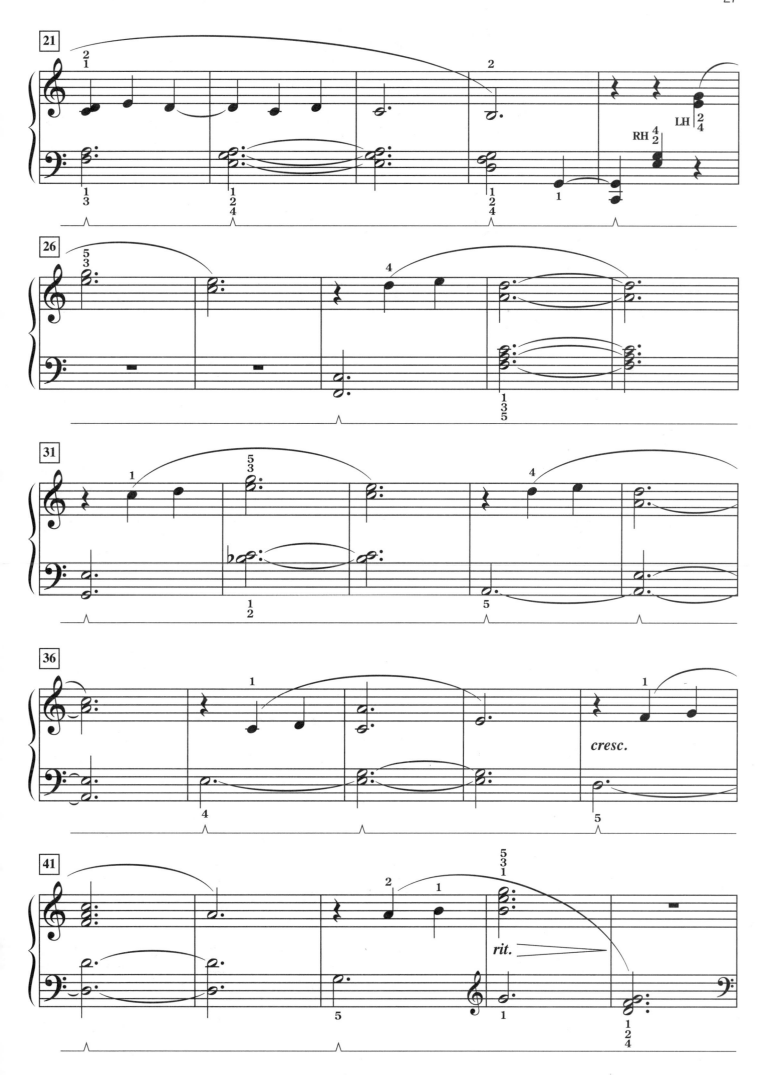

Maple Leaf Rag

Scott Joplin
Arranged by Carol Matz

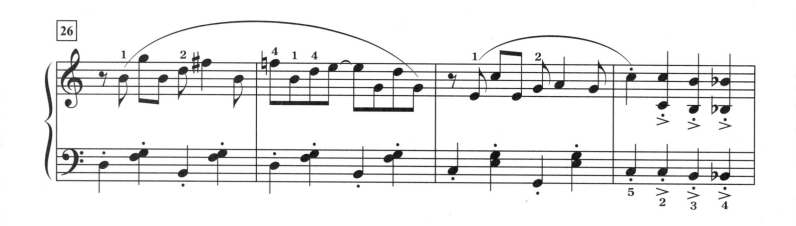

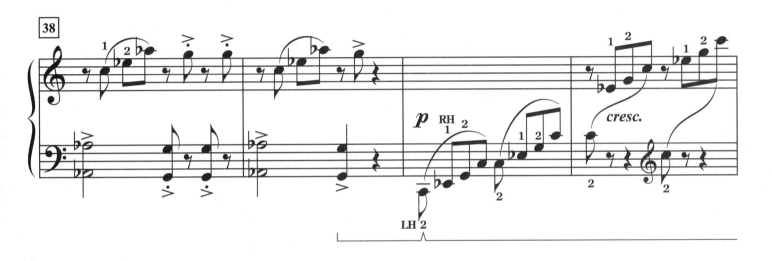

Alexander's Ragtime Band

Irving Berlin
Arranged by Carol Matz

Washington Post March

John Philip Sousa
Arranged by Carol Matz

- 3 counts each measure
38 - B♭ ξ E♭
♩ = 1 full count
fingering

The Star-Spangled Banner

Words by Francis Scott Key
Music by John Stafford Smith
Arranged by Carol Matz

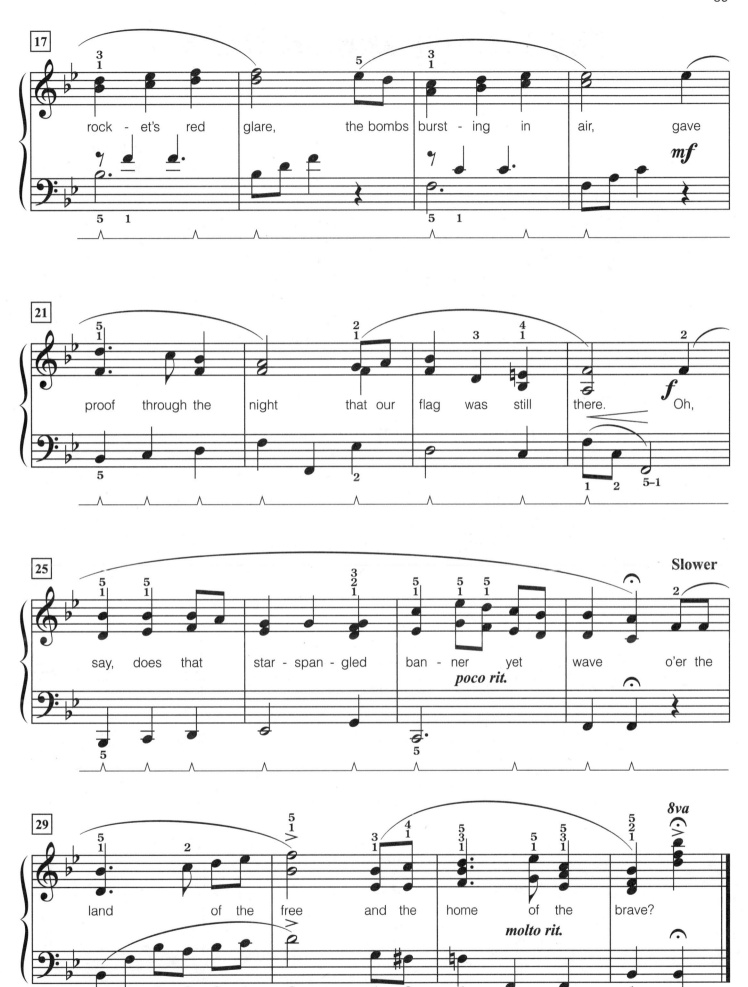

America

(My Country, 'Tis of Thee)

Traditional Melody
Words by Samuel F. Smith
Arranged by Carol Matz

* Top notes of left-hand octaves are optional.

Imagine

Words and Music by John Lennon
Arranged by Carol Matz

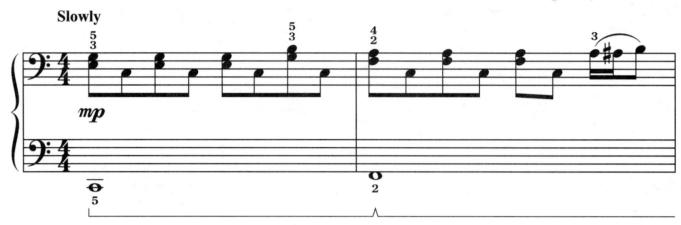

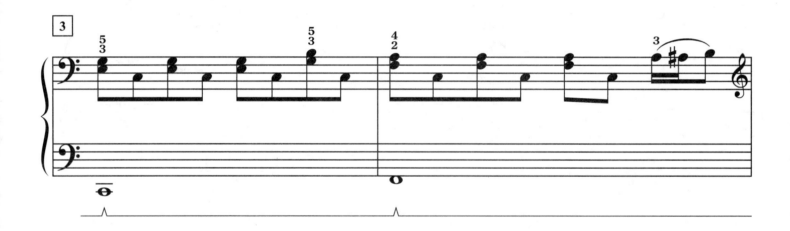

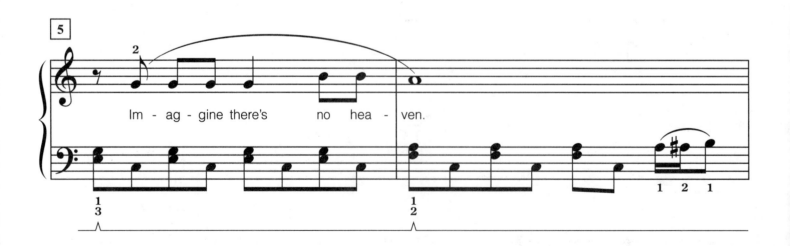

Im - ag - gine there's no hea - ven.

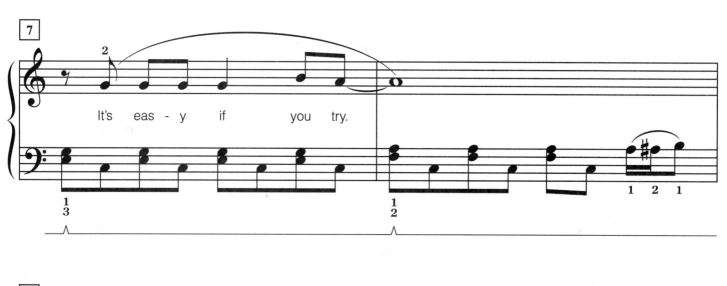

It's eas - y if you try.

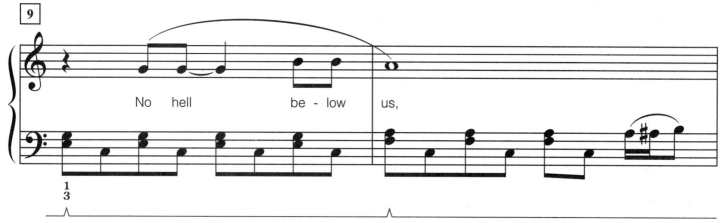

No hell be - low us,

a - bove us on - ly sky.   *mf* Im - ag - ine all the peo -

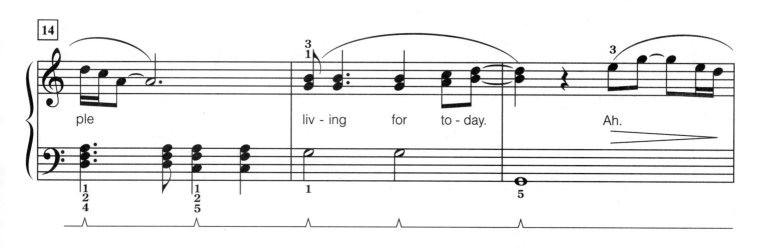

ple   liv - ing for to - day.   Ah.

* Play RH C the 1st time only.

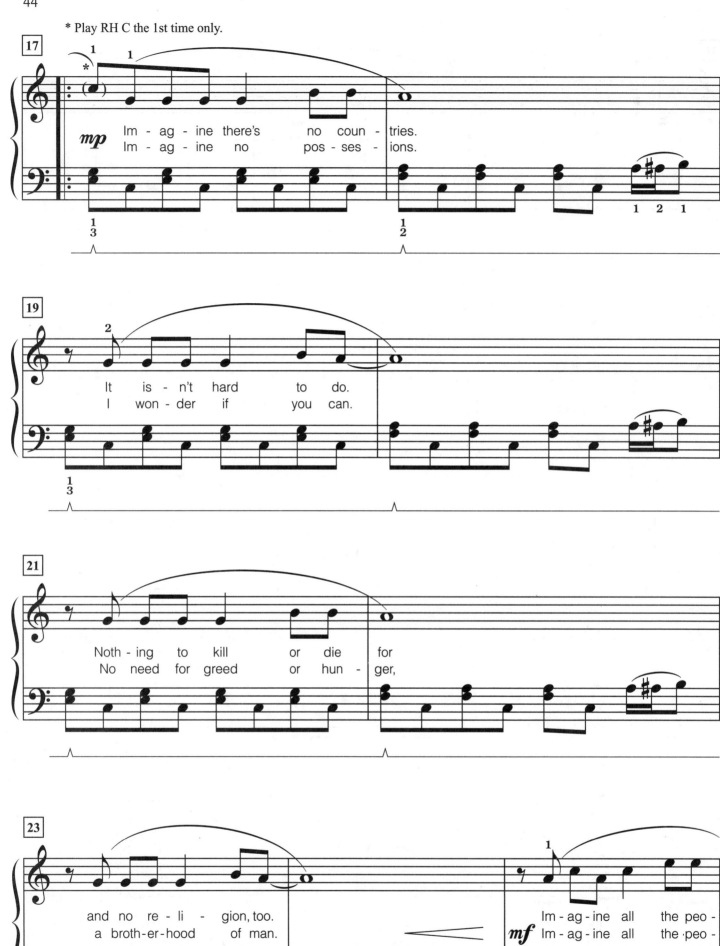

Eye of the Tiger

Words and Music by
Frankie Sullivan III and Jim Peterik
Arranged by Carol Matz

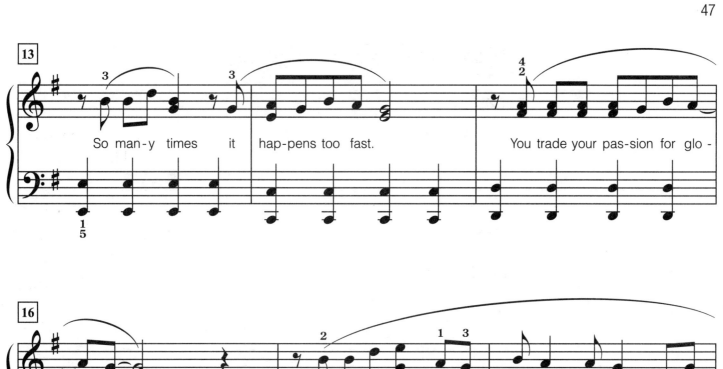

So man-y times it hap-pens too fast. You trade your pas-sion for glo -

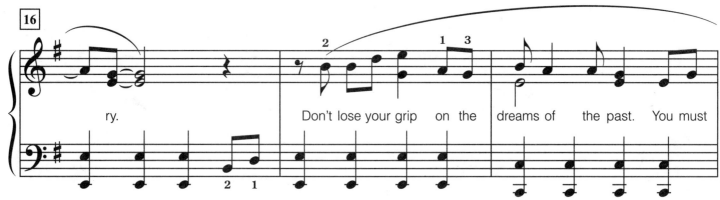

ry. Don't lose your grip on the dreams of the past. You must

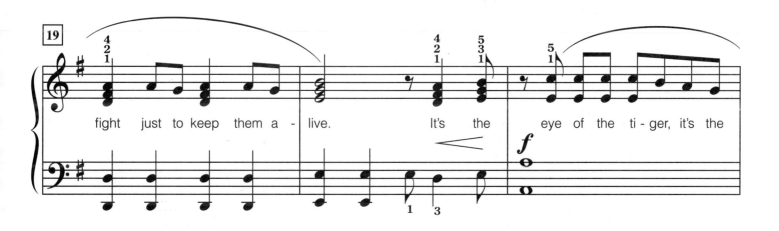

fight just to keep them a - live. It's the eye of the ti - ger, it's the

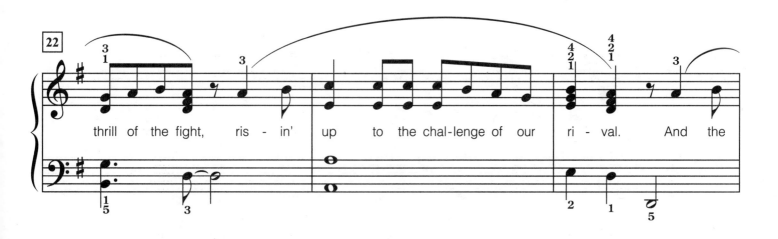

thrill of the fight, ris - in' up to the chal-lenge of our ri - val. And the

last known sur - vi - vor stalks his prey in the night, and he's watch - in' us all with the

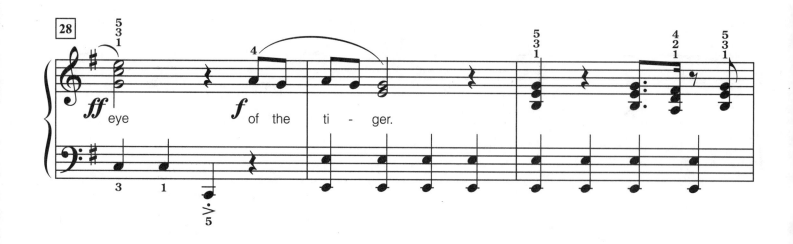

eye of the ti - ger.

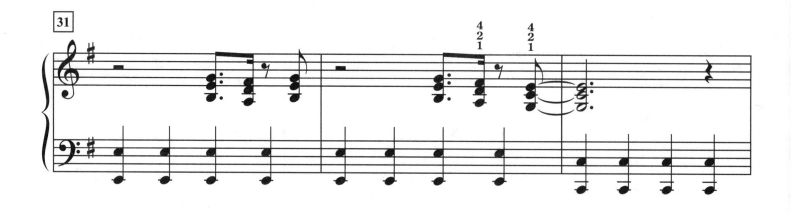

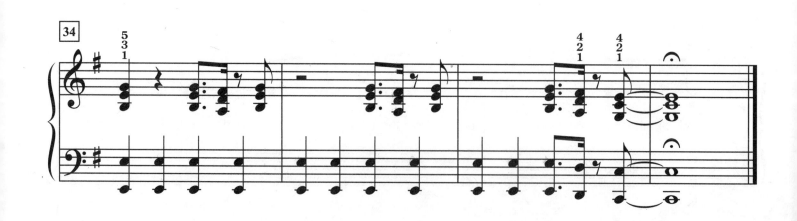

Don't Stop Believin'

Words and Music by Jonathan Cain,
Neal Schon and Steve Perry
Arranged by Carol Matz

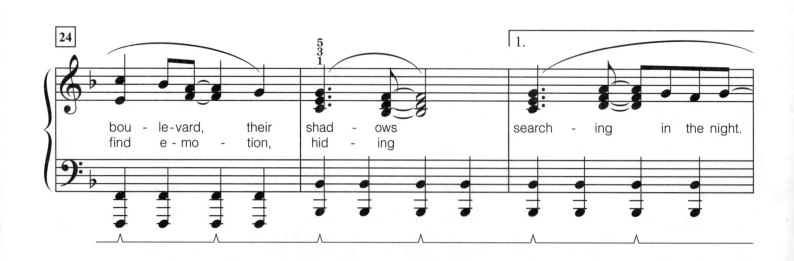

Musetta's Waltz

(from the opera *La bohème*)

Secondo

Giacomo Puccini
Arranged by Carol Matz

Musetta's Waltz

(from the opera *La bohème*)

Primo

Giacomo Puccini
Arranged by Carol Matz

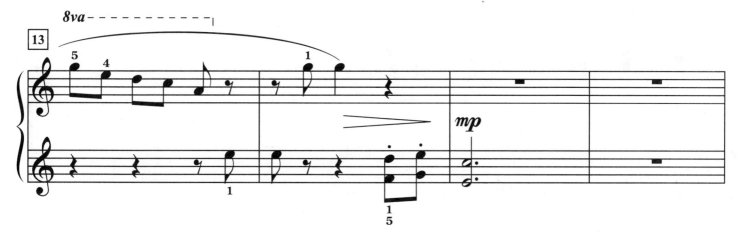

Secondo

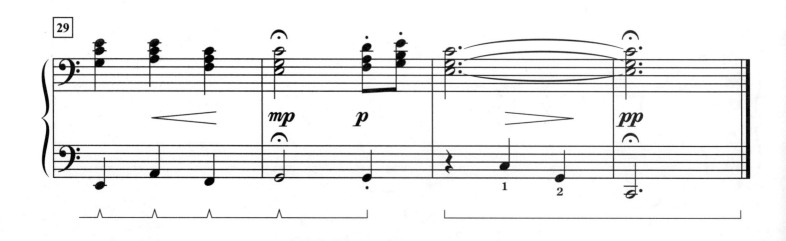

Primo

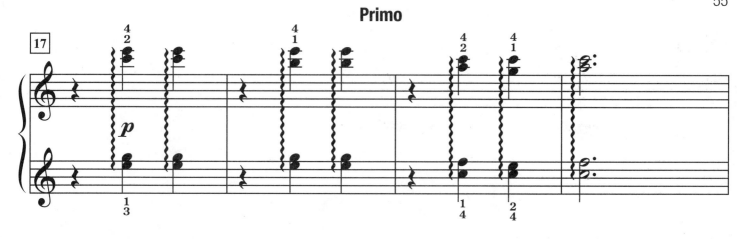

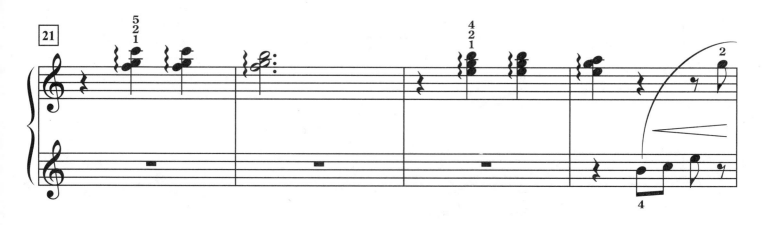

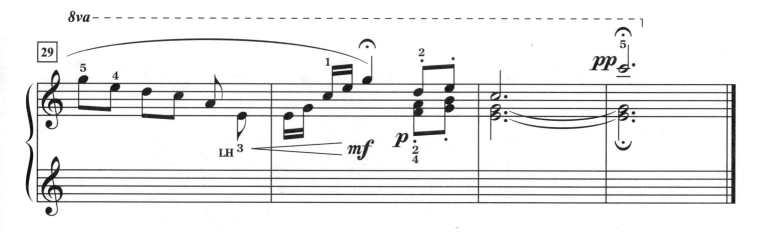

If I Only Had a Brain

(from *The Wizard of Oz*)

Secondo

Music by Harold Arlen
Lyrics by E.Y. Harburg
Arranged by Carol Matz

If I Only Had a Brain

(from *The Wizard of Oz*)

Primo

Music by Harold Arlen
Lyrics by E.Y. Harburg
Arranged by Carol Matz

Secondo

think of things I nev - er thunk be - fore,

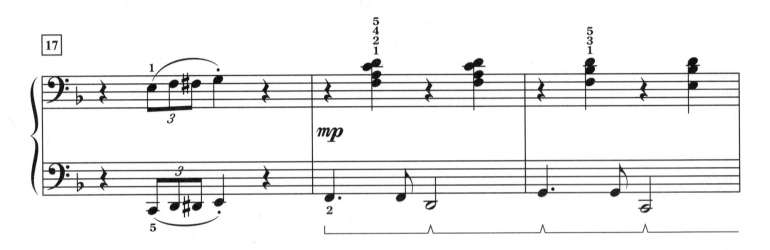

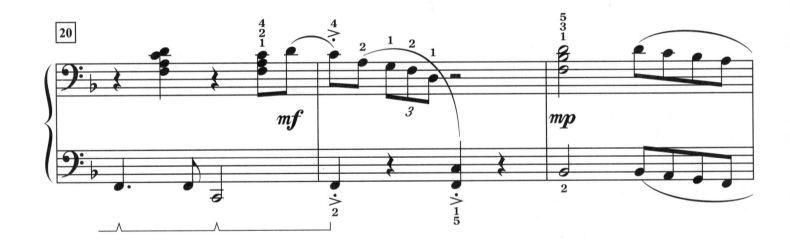

8va

Primo

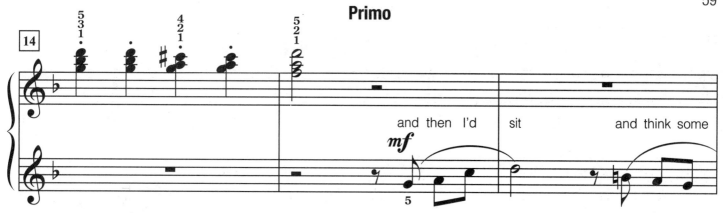

and then I'd sit and think some

more. I would not be just a nuf-fin', my head all full of stuf-fin', my

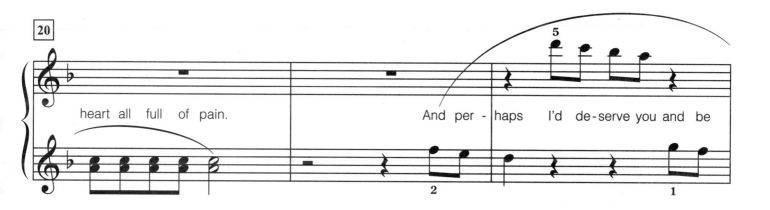

heart all full of pain. And per - haps I'd de-serve you and be

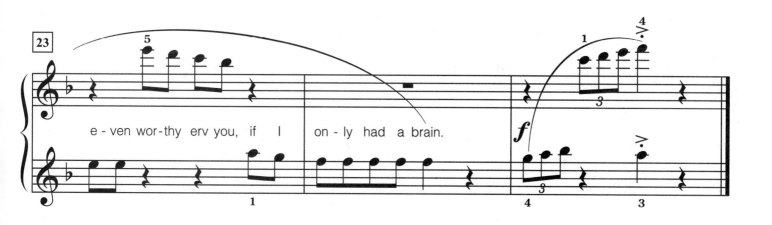

e - ven wor-thy erv you, if I on - ly had a brain.

James Bond Theme

Secondo

By Monty Norman
Arranged by Carol Matz

James Bond Theme

Primo

By Monty Norman
Arranged by Carol Matz

Secondo

Primo

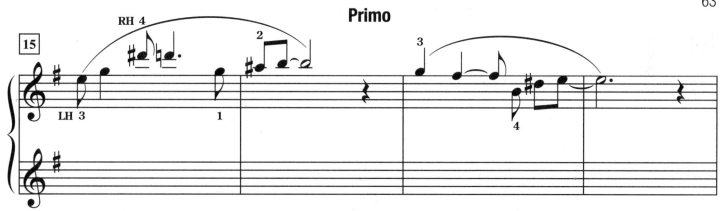

No swing